CULTIVATING CRITICAL THINKERS

CULTIVATING CRITICAL THINKERS

Strategies for Educators and Parents

AVERY NIGHTINGALE

Creative Quill Press

CONTENTS

CHAPTER 1

Introduction

First, as emerging adults transitioning from teenagers to adults, college students fare very well at critical thinking, as they work on the goals that matter to them. The problem is that schools are teaching students to try not to be wrong. Students need to be taught in a way that emphasizes how to think critically in the future, to contribute meaningfully to society. Thinking includes conceptual development, which supports student ability to think critically.

Increasingly, higher education professionals are realizing that they are producing students who can follow rules (or procedures) but who have not been taught to think critically. An emphasis on critical thinking over recall of facts can transform teaching, creating a more dynamic and student-centered environment. Despite broad consensus that critical thinking is important, educators are still defining it, and thus have not reached a consensus on what it means to cultivate it. In the context of developmental education, there are very few resources available on this topic. In this essay, I highlight several critical topics relating to critical thinking and the teaching of critical thinking.

CHAPTER 2

Importance of Critical Thinking

In the hierarchical scale of intellectual values, those at the apex confront and discuss ideas with respected authorities; professionals at the intermediate levels see surprising connections across seemingly diverse intellectual pursuits. At the base of the pyramid, students in elementary or middle level schools can be seen developing skills in "close observation," the ability to examine minutely and describe in rich detail, often using provocative perspectives. In adult conversations, we often hear echoes of rich understanding from early school experiences when students are able to differentiate visually and verbally propositions that are obviously false or completely true. It is essential to emphasize the significance of critical thinking at the elementary and middle school levels when young minds are maturing. Early exposure to lessons that promote the development of independent thinking produces adults who may actively participate in problem definition, search for information and voice opinions even when information is not immediately available.

"Must be 18 years of age to apply" is a familiar disclaimer posted in want ads and on most job descriptions. As career-hopeful college students frantically pursue their undergraduate studies, wonder turns to worry when they face this common job qualification. Curriculums offering majors in specific professional studies and the liberal arts are designed to augment students' education with courses and programs that inspire students from all disciplines to think critically and to develop intellectual values. Such a collaborative characteristic across the curriculum is highly regarded and scrutinized. Critical thinking skills help professionals in any field of study gather and synthesize information, evaluate its credibility, maintain an open-minded attitude and remain skeptical even if the "majority" endorses an idea.

CHAPTER 3

Understanding Critical Thinking Skills

Educational researchers, on the other hand, have struggled to differentiate critical thinking from other aspects of teaching. Some confusion still exists. Moreover, an agreement on what critical thinking actually encapsulates depends upon a variety of achievement and contextual factors, such as whether the research is inclusive or exclusive, and on the grade level of participants and whether that instruction is classroom or summer school-based. If those committed to critical thinking do not know what it is, or are unsure as to what makes critical thinkers actually good at thinking critically, then how are they to inspire, develop, and promote these essential skills in their learners?

When many people are asked to define "critical thinking", they might suffer a debilitating moment of terminology anxiety, as they can't come up with the "perfect" definition. There is reason for this. Some of the ambiguity comes from the fact that there has been a long-standing disagreement as to what exactly critical thinking entails and this has led to different understandings. Some of the ambiguity about the meaning of critical thinking comes from past perspective. For example, on a nominal level, which is where words are used in the absence of actual things to which they refer (referring to the word in and of itself), creative thinking is original, imaginative, innovative, and inventive in the way that life thought demands, and analytical thinking is active, informed, and inquiry-based thinking that emphasizes how data can be understood, integrated, and evaluated from the perspective of being objective and practically applied.

CHAPTER 4

Strategies for Educators

By supporting learners to develop new ideas, educators will notice that learners are capable of abstract, higher-order thinking and reasoning. By guiding learners through think-alouds (especially on the periphery of the multiple-task comparison triangle) and related practices, educators can also help learners to practice and develop these thinking skills and critical habits of mind. Noticing and then naming and reinforcing learner moves (actions and strategies) are important, too (e.g., "Oh, you just made a comparison between these two tasks! Do you notice that sometimes comparing two things can help you to better understand each one?"), as is providing opportunities for practice that will help learners to develop ownership of their emerging abilities and identities as critical thinkers.

As educators and parents, we want to help our students to think critically so that they can solve problems, make meaningful contributions to their communities, and understand that they have the power to make change in their own lives and the lives of others. Socratic seminar, or simply a Socratic discussion, is a structured method for holding a class dialogue... or small working group means. By providing a number of strategies such as think-alouds, and by supporting learners as they practice and develop their emerging critical thinking skills, educators can help learners of all ages and ability levels to think critically. Encourage learner metacognition and the idea that different perspectives bring about richer understandings. Learners can articulate their own thinking and learning processes, develop a metacognitive voice, and reflect on their attempts to answer questions such as "Does this make sense?" Relate to Growth Mindset work especially. This is particularly important for students who feel uncertain about engaging with the critical thinking process.

4.1. Encouraging Questioning

"Rather than believing that they know everything from that point [their question] on, teachers need to tap into that excitement. The 'stimulus' [the student's question) is the key to real education - an education that revolves around the things the student needs to know (or wants to understand) rather than what someone else believes they 'need to know at present'."

Close attention to one's questioning patterns is integral to the development of advanced critical thinking. By keeping track of the frequency with which we ask different types of questions, we develop an understanding of their most frequent modes. Stated differently, keeping a questioning log can help students become aware of a range of questioning strategies - strategies that accomplish a range of educational objectives. Indeed, the mother of critical thinking, Socratic questioning itself, manifests an inquisitive, data-gathering stance. Sudbury-based educator Roland Meighan writes:

Productive inquiry requires a supportive atmosphere that encourages students to question and participate actively in the learning process. Indeed, there are survey findings by the Higher Education Research Institute (HERI) about college students' first-year educational experiences that are relevant to students' questioning: classes emphasizing students' thinking and expression are the educational experiences most valued by students. Openness is the key word for the achievement of such an atmosphere - openness to new ideas, diversity, and what is new and different. The importance of this quality is vividly brought home through reading some of the numerous studies detailing students' experiences in traditional classrooms: there, students are relatively mute, with questions resembling something more like isolated, disconnected sounds than the line of questioning considered among social scientists to be indicative of critical thinking.

4.2. Promoting Analytical Thinking

We will mention different types of argument components that someone uses to bolster claims. We will discuss deductive and inductive reasoning to familiarize the difference and to emphasize the prioritizing nature of deductive reasoning. The goal will be to have students not only recognize the use of such points while in discussion or as found in their reading materials, but to include argument components when explaining or justifying their positions, introduce an argument component that our speaker remains true to during discussion or in their written composition, and to solely prioritize deductive reasoning to determine the validity of philosophical arguments.

Specific to reading, how we encourage students to engage with and respond to these materials fosters analytical thinking. Who does not like to know that their opinion is valued? Students are no different in suggesting their approval rating for offering their thoughts. But there is so much more to be gained when a teacher listens to students' ideas. By actively soliciting, considering the logic and value in their thoughts, a teacher models essential critical thinking skills for students and aids in their development of those same characteristics.

Encouraging analytical thinking is likely the most well-known approach to cultivating critical thinkers. To develop students' analytical capabilities, a teacher should introduce and promote the components that compose an argument and demonstrate the distinction between inductive and deductive reasoning. Incorporating argument analysis in the class curriculum is remarkably beneficial in helping students acquire this crucial form of thinking.

4.3. Teaching Problem-Solving Techniques

Helping students to develop qualities for good problem analysis requires helping them develop flexibility and facility in recognizing defense mechanism, understanding when they operate, and devising strategies for counteracting them. In order to develop this kind of reflective problem solving attitude we have to approach the problem solving instruction at fundamentally different levels by using an entirely different dulie. We have to develop attitudes for tolerance and patience, to face complexities in problem solving experiences, positive attitudes for frustration experienced during solution search, attitudes for open-mindedness, willingness to listen to other solutions, tolerance of pluralism existence, non-threatening attitudes to the fragile solutions of others, real perseverance and persistence to hang through solution search periods. How to develop tolerance to the frustration of solution search during problem solving experience is very important and very critical. Dependency and pseudo-dependency are detrimental to and contradictory to all these desirable attributes of good preparation and equipment for reflective, creative problem solving and reasoning capability, which we really seek them to have. When we are effectively making students capable of good problem solving, reflective thinking, research competence we have to think of good research habits, good research characters, good research behavior.

If the teacher is aiming to nurture skills for shaping a better society, then students need help in facing the complexities and integrative aspects of problems, in mapping out the areas of analysis, in dealing with emotional overtone, in judging and deciding values and courses of action. A few are prepared to take on such open-ended, messy problems. They are so used to the routine problems of their culture, the games and puzzle patterns, the closed systems, the ordered and delimited experiences that textbooks give and share. They have not tried to work on problems outside their field of textbook, subject matter routine, which they can work neatly and exhaustively, reapply known algorithms in such bounded, safe mini-ature situations. They do not experience the feeling of inadequacy, of uncertainty in their own values, and judgment capability. Since they have never cultivated criteria for problem solving in areas of feelings, values and judgments in dealing with problem data, they have never been sensitive to psychological trapdoors, to which indeed are the real cul-de-sacs of the "sudden idea" or the Aha-Erlebneiss. They do not develop this big problem solving incentive. They have the best aspirations, but they do not have the training for reflective thinking.

4.4. Fostering Open-Mindedness

Fostering open-mindedness complements the integration of curi-osities and skepticism. Consider revisiting the classroom "concept circle," but now with a focus on each being the center of the level for different aspects of pedagogy. See it as "our students and us" and again approach the Circle as being a kaizen-continuous improve-ment approach. Introduce structured, respectful dialogues that le-verage shared experiences or expose everyone to new perspectives and information. Understand that in reinforcing open-mindedness, we must instill points and levels of dialogue that respect differences while providing genuine critique when it is due. Remember that assessment requires creativity and originality. At times, informed skepticism, used up to a level of verified quality in original thoughts and assessments, becomes the content of teaching. Recognize that we can promote critical thinking instruction that values genuine dialogue between majoritarian and minoritarian discourse. We can promote individual judgment building and the appreciation for the witness of diversity. Never forget the potential of learning from differences in opinion.

Take a critical look at your own beliefs and ideas and model open-mindedness. Predict how passionate people are about their own beliefs and opinions and so accept you cannot change them, but you can show them others' experiences and what other people believe. This develops the students' nature of respect for all individuality and helps them stand up for individuality and difference in the world. Start with your own openness to other viewpoints, beliefs, and opinions. Practice acknowledging differences in perspectives and valuing them rather than judging them. People are often encouraged to listen to other perspectives merely for the sake of being polite or cordial, but we should strive to show genuine acceptance rather than mere tolerance. We should not be afraid of teaching the value of critical thinking to diverse audiences. We are doing a disservice to the next generation of critical thinkers if they are not aware of how to be skillful with their knowledge and respectful at the same time.

4.5. Enhancing Decision-Making Abilities

Being a competent decision-maker involves a type of reasoning that is both strategic and judgmental. It involves reasoning strategically in the following way: Here is an interesting question or issue. To decide what I should do, or what we should do, or what decision or position I should recommend, I will think of what I want to accomplish, and I will identify and evaluate options. I will take steps based on experience and rules of thumb to develop my own lists of options and what we should do, realizing that textbook solutions do not often apply!

One of the goals of thinking strategically and judgmentally is to give learners the skills they need to formulate desired outcomes (goals) and plan (in systematic ways) to reach them. Another goal is to develop their capacity to use analytical thinking and judgmental thinking skills to help them make defensible decisions, to think strategically no matter what the task they are engaged in or the issues they are facing. One way to help learners develop this capacity is to teach them to be skilled decision-makers.

CHAPTER 5

Strategies for Parents

When parents ask their children how their day at school was, the typical answer is, "fine." Many parents express their frustration about how difficult it is to get their children to tell them anything about their day. A proactive way to engage children and get them to talk is to tell them in advance what you are looking forward to talking about. For example, "I can't wait to eat dinner and hear three great things that happened today!" If the question-answer format doesn't work right away, try using an activity such as drawing or playing with play dough to get your child talking. Limiting the use of electronic devices at home is another way to open up channels of communication. Create zones in the house that are "device free" where, as a family, you can engage in conversation. Allow the child to use a communication device (a smart phone, for example) with the expectation that if a text comes in from you during that time, that he/she will respond to it.

As parents, we want our children to think critically: to analyze, question, and think creatively and independently. Throughout our children's educational careers, we have heard that there is more to true education than passing standardized tests and having the ability to remember facts temporarily. In order to become productive citizens and socially engaged individuals, children must be able to think critically. To cultivate critical thinkers, both our children's teachers and we, their parents, need a variety of strategies to develop these skills in a way that is developmentally appropriate. Here are some ideas for how to encourage our children to become independent thinkers that promote their questioning, and challenge them to see the world through different perspectives.

5.1. Creating a Supportive Environment

(7) 'Question' becomes the last stage.

(6) 'Choose' or the vote comes in as the vote of discussion and being or the final choice following personalized judgments.

(5) 'Debate' is the stage of conversation associated with giving and finding reasoning with the intention of convincing others of the merits of a standpoint.

(4) 'Discuss' or argue is the phase that is contingent on the previous or the 'listening' phase and is aimed at explanation construction.

(3) Integrate the 'listen' phase so that views and opinions of different students are equally acknowledged by allowing them to utter their ideas, attitudes, beliefs, or assumptions in the open arena.

(2) Engage students in the 'thinking process' by encouraging students to take questions with a challenge and to put time and effort into coming up with answers that they believe in.

1. Be clear about what abilities and skills teachers expect their students to develop or acquire. Similarly, teachers should have a clear understanding of what features will be characteristic of their product (i.e., those same abilities and skills in the student body).

   There are seven components necessary for teachers to create an environment in a class that supports critical thinking.

These are (please note that the article is using the original 7-stage model: think, listen, discuss, debate, choose, question, and enrich):

Creating a community or a culture, whether in the classroom or at home, that supports critical and creative thinking helps promote an environment that fosters intellectual risk-taking. A supportive environment has been shown to have a direct relationship to the higher cognitive performance of students. Beneficial learning environments are ones that encourage questions by students rather than having a teacher dominating the class space. In fact, encouraging questions and issues from students has been shown to increase higher-level thinking as mirrored by the students' cross-examination of the knowledge and the knowledge-generating process. This higher-level thinking has been promoted when the students are engaged in debate and not where the teacher is using a lecture mode.

5.2. Engaging in Thought-Provoking Conversations

We need to ask good questions in order to encourage higher-order thinking from our students. Indeed, the main reason for asking a question is to collect a piece of information, but there are many questions that will never develop an inquisitive mind. Knowledge has to be connected in some way. Although the regular curriculum must be taught, it is still possible to make time for these types of discussion-based questions, particularly when some of the alternative assignments or scripted examples are implemented in place of those requiring multiple-choice, procedural fluency tasks. Depending on the course length, these can be as short as ten minutes, or as long as an entire hour, or full class period.

A student's problem-solving performance is enhanced in direct relation to the amount of instruction designed to provide for thinking about thinking. Students can quickly learn that while problems have right answers, they can learn something without the right answer by trying to effectively explain their reasoning and by questioning the reasoning of their classmates. Fostering an environment for higher-order thinking can be a daunting task for all of us, especially when we feel so overwhelmed by time and syllabus constraints. The ideal environment for critical thinking will occur in a space for shared inquiry that can be nurtured whenever an individual's concerns about the truth, reasonability, or significance of the ideas brought forth are made evident.

5.3. Encouraging Independent Thinking

First, while there is significant utility to be found in methods to cultivate critical thinkers, there is unmistakable irony too. The very concept suggests a rather conservative and traditional orientation. Instead of perpetuating convention, therefore, it seems more in keeping with the spirit of cultivating critical thinkers to put a continually emergent spin on things. Some possibilities are as follows: use the chain of questioning (sometimes referred to as the Socratic method) often and publicly to disrupt preformed patterns. It is my opinion that altering the format and the grounds of the question to be of surprise would inspire a higher level of alertness among students for critical thinking. Further, I believe it would reduce the chances of the question-dodging tactics which currently evade the perturbations of the conventional educational context.

Cultivating Critical Thinkers: Strategies for Educators and Parents is an excellent summary of some methods useful in the cultivation of critical thinkers in the classroom. In the main, the subject is deep and deserving of fuller and further consideration. With that in mind, this response hopes to critically extend the issue from a complementary perspective.

I will try to accomplish this by considering relationships between enlarging the ability of others to think critically, confining educational practices, and the role of the educator in institutional contexts as well as larger social systems. In the end, some conclusions are provided.

5.4. Exposing to Diverse Perspectives

In order to develop these important qualities in our students and children, we must be mindful of the attitudes that teachers or parents demonstrate in their judgment, decision-making, interpretation, evaluation, problem-solving, research, discussion, and communication. Children and students often take these attitudes as a model. It is important to present information about how people from various socio-cultural backgrounds interpret and represent the same situation differently. This helps them understand the subjective nature of reality and the fact that it does not correspond to a single, broad reality. Our students should also be encouraged to develop high intellectual responsibility in every area, from science to literature, from history to the arts, during their primary and secondary education.

A proverb states, "When in Rome, do as the Romans" to emphasize the importance of adapting to one's environment. However, a critically thinking person should instead follow the example of wise Romans. Therefore, educators and parents must teach and model the important knowledge associated with being intelligent, wise, and successful citizens of the world. These individuals are well-informed world citizens who are open-minded, fair, honest, ethically sound, skilled, and knowledgeable in their field. They also possess self-awareness, inner spirit, self-evaluating ability, the ability to obtain, interpret, and process information, evaluate information, communicate critical opinions, make informed decisions, have analytical and problem-solving skills, and are capable of effective information management.

5.5. Providing Opportunities for Decision-Making

A critical thinker is motivated and capable of regulating the learning process by setting personal task objectives or choosing alternate means of task mastery. Without opportunities to make decisions about the learning process, there is no reason for students to think critically about their learning or the metacognitive processes used to regulate their learning. In order to foster the development of students' metacognitive processes educators need to provide opportunities for independent thought surrounding the evaluation of task demands, an examination of the interaction between attitudinal and cognitive strategies, as well as meaningful use of self-regulated learning processes critical thinking and student self-regulation should be nurtured by providing situations where decisions are constantly required in the organization, regulation, and evaluation of the learning process in order to foster the understanding of self-regulated learning.

Given the current emphasis on multiple intelligences, experiential education, and the importance of learning to be scientists, it seems surprising that order is still popular as a means of keeping children quiet, particularly since research into student motivation has emphasized the importance of autonomy and a sense of independence. This may, however, reflect society's, and particularly schools', concerns with the control and management of students and staff. This misinterpretation of the importance of order as a precursor to independent thought represents a paradox, since it is essential for educators to teach students how to think independently and foster an understanding of the self-regulated learning processes they are expected to use, particularly since little research has been conducted in the use and development of self-regulated learning.

Assessing Critical Thinking Skills

Educational researchers agree that critical thinking is a skill that can be learned and taught through planned and systematic application of methods and strategies for critical thinking. However, the research across all academic disciplines suggests that many factors other than those courses have an effect on critical thinking abilities. For example, Danby and Lee found significant increases in critical thinking skills at the fifth and seventh grade levels after students have completed a cross-curricular unit in critical thinking at the Dreyfus Intermediate School of the East Ramapo Central School District, which included five classes and several skills that were taught as organized within the planned instruction. This suggests critical thinking is an ongoing process that can be developed over time. Kelly and Salinas explored potential factors that have an effect on the development of critical thinking abilities and found that planned interventions modestly, if at all, increase the critical thinking abilities of undergraduate students. A common post-secondary relationship mechanism posits that a student's last school attended will have an effect on future work while Calver, Armor-Davis, Lockheed-Martin, Els, and Kelly propose that planned intervention is important but through its development of a student's ability to engage in assessment of different aspects of their life. Kelly and Salinas offer several potential components of the learning environment (college) that could magnify the affective and cognitive development of critical thinking and critical reasoning skills. The majority of the papers that report the results of programs aimed at improving critical thinking focus on the educational challenge from a high school or college and university perspective. Notable works in critical thinking that include assessment measures have typically taken the form of critical thinking work at the college level to bolster critical thinking skills. The research in critical thinking has crossed a variety of topics that include critical thinking skills, understanding of complex thinking processes, predictions, prescriptions and selections, critical thinking dispositions, and deductive reasoning.

6.1. Developing Effective Assessment Methods

A motivating factor for students to engage in critical thought will be if there is extrinsic motivation to put in that added effort, especially for topics that increase uncertainty such as those requiring critical thinking. In the attempt to best prepare students to collaborate and meaningfully contribute in the many environments based on innovations based on new knowledge, grading practices that use behavioral objectives discourage going beyond the standards even if there is evidence that 'exceeding... objectives over time improves both retention and comprehension". While there can be potential drawbacks in providing students with reasons why a task is effective, it can provide students with reasons why putting in the extra effort is worthwhile. Thinking beyond education, anyone who uses any system for any length of time knows what is effective and what is not. In many of today's systems, we will act in ways that optimize "a known variable, even if it is less important than an unknown variable. When penalty is certain, but probability and size of rewards are uncertain, it becomes a reasonable general maxim to not try if the most likely outcome is poor. So of course for today's students, certainly most known variables are external rewards, such as the standard 'rewards' of society in terms of net worth, academic scores, social networks or the "high-risk high-reward offer" included in most television reality and game shows. Misreadings of the last error can occur only if a student cannot calculate odds. Becoming critical about irrelevant rewards given by society is an advance in one's critical thought. When one is unable to calculate the odds, necessary outcomes cannot be responsible and the thinking is not effective.

Assignments that are going to cultivate critical thinking in students need to be challenging and interesting, both to the student and the teacher. How is one to ensure that they have designed such a learning experience? Dewey wrote, "A curriculum may be criticized as being either too easy or too hard. On the first criticism it gets 'soft'. On the second it gets 'stuffed'." Considerations of assessments that can influence effort, the creation of assignments that are transparent through rubrics and frequent assessments, will be discussed. Finally, what sense can be made of course evaluations is a final topic.

6.2. Observing and Documenting Critical Thinking Behaviors

Given inaccuracies associated with memory, surveys, and interviews, we are most confident about noting higher order thinking behaviors when we observe them. We have been collecting observational data in multiple classes for several years using an ethogram that describes critical thinking and an instrument that categorizes entries on the ethogram, differentiating behavior indicative of higher order thinking from behavior indicative of superficial thinking. Instruction targets for the research included critical thinking, or the products of critical thinking. Results showed that for the majority of the 20 categories, more instructional targets (ITs) reflecting higher order thinking (ITCategory 3) occurred in a single class period in group education classes than in any other class type. Further, results despite the observation of group education classes occurring after individual education and hands-on classes suggests a preparation effect such that students learn more complex material in group than in individual education classes.

Facione and his colleagues provided a lengthy list of behaviors that may be indicative of critical thinking. Among these examples of critical thinking behavior are: analyzing arguments or information, identifying values and preconceptions in arguments or information, judging the validity, credibility, and relevance of arguments and information, considering other viewpoints, constructing logical and compelling arguments or information, recognizing contradictions, conclusions, answers, or theses, and identifying unstated assumptions. Since critical thinking is assessing and interpreting knowledge and dispositions, we must assess and interpret the behavior we observe. The following examples were taken from personal communications with a former student who observed one of the authors (NRC) in the classroom and one of the criteria from Facione's critical thinking assessment almost verbatim (the complete table with examples appears in the appendix).

6.3. Analyzing Critical Thinking Performance

In addition, we have observed that the volume of homework delivered in the semester's second part has significantly grown in both courses. It resulted in arriving at a point that the development of the analysis skill direction difference was negative i.e. student's performance initially has predominantly moved to a weak performance and stayed mostly there. Finally, in this work, we have presented a comprehensive research over the project-centered critical thinking and program and, thus, proved that an approach through project-based learning can be efficiently applied despite the many traditional claims opposing it, especially taking into account the format of the critical thinking classes.

The last component of a critical thinking class is focused on the development of critical thinking. We have analyzed the general directional cognitive changes (both in terms of the weak and strong performance) of students based on the California Critical Thinking Disposition Inventory (CCTDI). It is interesting to continue this research by analyzing the development of specific skills a course student receives. The difference between performance in the first and the last critical thinking class shows 2 significant opposite results. On the one hand, skills of finding arguments have not improved much and predominantly moved to a strong performance direction, what can be good as many college classes one day can deliver too much information in too short time so a student sometimes should perform some analyses based on not so strong judgment. On the other hand, the skills of analysis and deduction are, vice versa, moved to predominantly weak performance, or have significantly developed in a negative direction.

6.4. Providing Constructive Feedback

In addition to project feedback, classes also include forms of feedback through questioning, which are more instructional in nature and used to guide conversations toward certain subjects in CT. Asking questions the responses to which will engage students in more sophisticated thinking can provide a good scaffold for CT growth. (Questions can also be contextually sensitive, tailored to provoke a certain kind of response from a particular student.) By asking new questions and providing guidance in response to student inquiries, teachers can further CT in a collective manner. For example, instructors can try referring back to earlier points in discussion, a way to move forward with the topic at hand without ignoring earlier comments. These strategies work well for teachers who are good active listeners because they have developed an exceptional ability to focus on the responses they hear, consider what the students bring to the discussion, and examine their ideas in some depth so that they can appreciate how these can be refined and expanded. These classrooms are centered around mentoring. This allows teachers to: (1) take advantage of the interactive nature of CT; (2) build classes in a way that advances CT as a collaborative process; and (3) help students achieve success by acknowledging their past accomplishments. At the center of the cultivation of critical thinking (CT) is feedback from the teacher. Constructive feedback is seen as a fundamental aspect of developing CT, a form of teaching that is both constructivist (i.e., a two-way interaction between teacher and student) and teacher-guided (i.e., the teacher serves as the facilitator, guiding the student's understanding during this interaction). Of particular value for the student is feedback that engages, is didactic, and provides the evaluator with important information about a student's work. Didactic feedback is reflective in nature, offering essential guidance that the student can use to gain a better understanding of a subject. A constructive evaluation is positive, pointing out strengths and areas of improvement; it respects each effort made by the student and provides clearly articulated and detailed direction about how the student's work could be improved. An important dimension of feedback is how it is delivered. Instructors should take great care to frame their feedback in ways that orient their interactions around results of the assessment (e.g., student work) and not the student.

Integrating Critical Thinking into Curriculum

Mathematical problems and examples work much better if they are presented as real-world problems to solve. Critical education literature points out how students are bored with a meaningless presentation of course content, and that it causes teaching to be challenging. I once had a student yell out, as he left, "When will we learn something useful?" Use of the applied material has been found to increase the interest and involvement of students. Whenever possible, examples used in the classroom should be directly tied to real-world applications. However, an example tied to the everyday is no savior from criticism of students who are sensing that the course content has been co-opted by ideology. Extractions may not lead to real problems that intrigue the minds of students. Engaging students is much more than having interesting facts that are applied to teach known course content. Infusion method is different from the application of otherwise sterile content. Curricular changes typically restore sterile examples while new courses often create the paltry.

Integrating critical thinking skills into the classroom or in on-line discussions is fairly easy for a teacher to do. Teaching critical thinking skills does not necessarily necessitate a commitment to a new or more specialized set of courses or numerous lectures. The mundane can be pressed into service to encourage critical inquiry. The following suggestions can be used to develop critical thinking: use examples that illustrate only the concept being taught in the textbook. Critical thinking is limited by the crummy examples from the textbooks where concepts are presented. Elementary mathematics often provides students with problems to solve that have really no other purpose than to teach that skill. Developing a course with no textbook may be impractical and usually an issue of external review by faculty and the administration. Instead, examples that are used should be selected from the textbook. Any example that is used should illustrate the concept being presented.

7.1. Identifying Key Concepts for Critical Thinking

Based on the Ontario Ministry of Education's curriculum, and Beardslee's curriculum of critical thinking skills, researchers and experienced educators currently involved in the teaching of critical thinking were presented with the question "In your opinion and experience, what types of critical thinking can and should be taught to students from kindergarten to Grade 5"? Researchers coded participant responses. As a first step towards creating curriculum guidelines for the teaching of critical thinking at the elementary school level, this research will be used to identify key concepts before ranking them in order of importance. Particular recommendations for classroom implementation, teacher education, and future research directions will also be explored in greater detail.

The consensus in critical thinking research is that we should be teaching critical thinking at the elementary school level. Teaching critical thinking at the elementary school level can be very difficult, however. Consequently, it is important to identify the key concepts to be taught to ensure students are able to develop the skills required for critical thinking. This research identifies 55 different pieces to the critical thinking puzzle that can be taught from kindergarten through Grade 5.

7.2. Designing Engaging Learning Activities

Consider teaching students to list pros and cons by having them play a structured coin flipping game. To play, you need an evaluator and two opposing teams. The evaluator flips the coin, and Team A immediately decides whether they are "Pro" the outcome or "Con" the outcome, and they then strategize about the best reasons for their justified position. After 2 minutes, the evaluator stops the discussion by announcing which side of the coin is facing upwards. If it is heads, Team B insists that Team A did not do a good job—had the coin landed tails, they would have been able to argue equally well for a different position. At this point, Team B persuasively lists plausible opposite reasons. Facts, ethical principles, or irresistible theoretical claims that are capable of bridging opinions are useful. It is useful to encourage values like fairness, inclusivity, and kindness. This can be done by rendering Team A the evaluators in the next round, or through discussions after each round.

The chapters in this book have defined critical thinking as an ability to recognize problems, open-mindedly explore their elements and nature, and then work towards a well-founded, supported solution. Since thinking emerges in social relationships and with the use of languages, we must engage our students and children within a problem-centered, dialogical pedagogical environment in which we constantly work to see things from their point of view, respond to their questions, and start discussions. Also necessary for developing critical thinkers are interesting learning activities that enable students to discover and openly question complexities, begin to discover alternative perspectives, and discuss the merits of these perspectives through critical dialogue. For effective learning, our activities must generate student interest: two of the most effective ways to actively engage students are through the creation of games and simulations.

7.3. Incorporating Real-World Problem Solving

2. In attempting to expose college students to the challenges of real-world problem solving, I have used two strategies. The first strategy attempts to uncover critical thinking skills that

students bring with them to an "Exploration Physics" course for nonphysics majors. Its validity is based on the assumption that some hint of future critical thinking activity can be discerned in current educational activities and personality traits, for example, a willingness to take an unexpected yet beneficial next step in the problem-solving process. For this experiment, students in 53 college classes were asked on the first day of class to participate in an approach that was disguised in the form of a speed game. Each student was shown a picture that contained no human figures. In an apparently whimsical exercise, students were asked to examine the personless picture and with increasing confidence identify the picture's location. This seemingly peculiar request carefully followed the predictions of string theory, a theory that unifies all elementary particles with gravity.

1. Connections to real-world problems let students appreciate the relevance of content and motivate them to learn that content. Therefore, when faculty teach courses in their area of specialization, they should show how their subject matter applies to some facet of day-to-day life. But regardless of the discipline taught, real-world problem solving is an educational approach that nicely fits the skills of a critical thinker. Unfortunately, fostering the latter three kinds of questions with supportive feedback and instruction too often is viewed primarily as a set of skills that can be learned. In search of an efficient shortcut to the problem, critical thinking training is omitted or greatly reduced in significance. While some student improvement might occur as a result of the other modes of instruction, little, if any increase in critical thinking is likely to occur as well.

7.4. Encouraging Collaboration and Discussion

Critical thinking can be most effective when all educational systems - home, school, and community - take on the mission, using a coherent, consistent approach that encourages learners to think for themselves. The systems must develop resources that make it possible for caregivers to impart the values and gifts of their community in their children. The second most important factor involves resources provided by educators to help learners become critical thinkers and problem solvers. Not only do leaders want and need these thinking and learning attributes to develop, learning citizens require them in a republican "enterprise educational environment," one where individuals will engage as thoughtful contributors or academic citizens in most, and perhaps every, aspect of everyday life.

Collaboration can also help with reading between the lines and denotation (recognizing and understanding systems of meaning). Techniques like Socratic seminars and group discussion can help learners to make their literacy development visible and to use their improving skills with increasingly complex and advanced texts. Keeping a class journal is another method that can be used to assess students' level of learning and literacy development, while also creating a record that can be returned to again and again. Educators can model the behavior they wish to see in actual parental and/or guardian behavior, serving as an example of effective questioning and solution development.

CHAPTER 6

Overcoming Challenges in Cultivating Critical Thinking

In the age of standardized tests, we "must remember that mandates at all levels of education have changed curriculum focus in the classroom, often times requiring teachers to teach state test skills rather than teach subject area content material utilizing effective pedagogical strategies which can facilitate growth in critical thinking." Each grade level and every content area demands a series of specific well-thought-out strategies, principles and techniques which help balance the reality of teaching the subject matter with the necessity of infusing thinking skills into the instruction. Another concern being faced is that teachers often feel uncomfortable with the instruction of critical thinking skills. An essential feature of ensuring a practical model for effective thinking instructions is to assist teachers to develop confidence, competence, and comfort, contributing to improving problem-solving skills. We want to establish greater benefits for teachers and students across the continuum of prekindergarten through postsecondary modules. Simply blitzing teachers with innumerable thinking strategies or inundating teachers with information about critical thinking can result in negative outcomes unless performed with a modicum of balance (i.e., acknowledging trepidations and concerns of many educators).

Another challenge is the issue that many teachers and parents lack the time and resources to embrace the well-established database of critical thinking strategies, principles, and techniques. Since teachers consider their time to be extremely valuable, they will be most receptive to strategies that have been designed specifically, efficiently, and effectively to promote critical thinking skills in their students. There is "no action research strategic model that engages students that can be more valuable than those that instigates and excites students' creativity, curiosity, and respect of learning; produces critical problem-solving minds; develops the skills of reasoning as well as evaluative skills; cultivates deep reflective learners.

Educators and parents face many challenges in imparting education, emphasizing the cultivation of critical thinking. One challenge is addressing the pre-service and in-service professional development of teachers, helping educators understand the importance of critical thinking and providing them with the strategies, principles, and techniques that cultivate higher-order thinking skills in the classroom. Moreover, many teachers have not experienced model critical thinking curricula or instructional practices in their own educations. School administrators and policy makers are urged to create opportunities for teachers to develop these important skills by helping them to gain an education that will benefit the children they teach. This education includes examining the purposes of postsecondary education, different ways of teaching, critical thinking curriculum (and curriculum materials), and pedagogy that enable effective classroom strategies for fostering higher-order thinking skills.

8.1. Addressing Resistance to Change

Reframing our perspectives concerning educational change may assist our personal and collective empowerment and alleviate feelings of hopelessness or anger that accompany failed tentative steps. When discussing educators' concerns over the powerful repercussions of the political climate, recognizing the social realities and power structures that limit our positions as educators, but emphasizing educators' responsibility to transcend these limitations through professional awareness, development, and involvement in curricular decisions. Also highlighted these responsibilities concerning advocacy and justice: "There is a clarion call for educators to become critical pedagogues who can foster awareness of the larger social worlds in which learners live, who can offer support through teachable moments, and who can establish the language that links the heart to legislative action". To assist educators and parents with that call, we offer fifteen suggested strategies tailored for ease of identification and implementation and more readily adopted as components of professional development.

Although we appreciate and understand the resistance to and fear of change felt by today's parents and teachers, the task of educating students for their future, to help them realize and utilize their unique potentials, demands new paradigms and methodologies, and we suggest a shift in perspective that may impact feelings of power and motivation regarding those changes. We advocate a more active mindset toward maneuvering within that optimistic perspective. Passive acceptance of or resistance against change limits our power of influence over directions within a particular new paradigm, and unfortunately this rigidity often leads to stereotypes concerning correct practices, rigid dogmas, and limits to our intellectual depth when examining our students' own complexities. In the present educational climate these constraints, we argue, may further cripple the functioning of educational systems. If we acknowledge and adopt actively the roles of innovators and researchers of curricular and instructional strategies, then we may redirect our critical thinking abilities into practical submissions for the gaze of public scrutiny and implementation toward the realization of our fundamental objectives with the whole child. We are called, he argued, to strip away the layers of superficial knowledge, to search our own depths for higher-order questions, and to motivate professional response through kindness, insight, concern for students and their families, and respect.

8.2. Supporting Students' Emotional Development

This is a seemingly intractable problem, but lessons from psychology may help to resolve it. For example, Matsuba and Walker (2005) found that when students experience competition, they feel that their self-worth is at stake and hence are hypervigilant to possible failures and less willing to consider new or worthy ideas. Conversely, Theysler and Stevens (2000) found that cooperative structures generated the feeling of security and hence free to adopt and test and revise the ideas of others, because more joust. In the same vein, Burnett et al. (2013) found that the use of open-ended problems designed to demonstrate care for the individual student helped to foster a sense of autonomy and therefore improved the students' ability to express their implicit or explicit knowledge. More specifically related to argumentation, Walton and not only found the ties that provide ideologies and respect for diverse perspectives, but he emphasized the importance of employing these characteristics in peer dialogues. The empowerment also seems to be particularly important for the learning and development of students in general and Wilson (2016) pointed out, the excitement and the enthusiasm that students experience in cultivating their curiosities and the use of news platforms could increase these opportunities.

Whether you choose to instill the joy of discovery, cultivate a growth mindset, or teach argumentation, cultivating critical thinkers also requires you to create an educational environment that is emotionally supportive. The cultivation of critical thinkers may be for naught if they are not willing to take intellectual risks, whether that means asking for help when needed, advocating for their own point of view, or embracing the belief that they can engage in debates with various topics, generating many adoptions arguments, and sequentially test and revise those arguments. These are not simple or easy tasks. Students may be afraid to take intellectual risks or may even view asking for help as a form of cheating because they have hyper-competitive motivations. Students who do not respect diverse points of view and instead see argumentation as a verbal jousting match may instead feel that arguing leads to social isolation: if I argue against our friend's views, then no one will want to hang out with me. Bold and concomitant findings are the following:

8.3. Dealing with Information Overload

If, according to the law of minimal and substantial distances, paying attention means acting as though there could be an arrival zone for purposeful behavior, selection is undoubtedly required. The perceptual system does not operate as a passive, and overall data acquisition, data-categorization, or global comparison system (the "spectator"); rather it is constantly conducting targeted comparisons. In real life, some old familiar demonstrations can remind us of the operating principles of our perception (this is the case of the genuine figure/ground reversal of two-dimensional images, which demonstrates the salience weighting assigned to what should be perceived).

Now that we are all swamped with information, one of the most important goals for the development of a thinking individual appears to be knowing how to sift the essential from the nonessential, understanding that paying attention involves the identification of scarce time resources. This allows us to better predict immediate contextual reactions and select necessary assessment strategies that may need revising on the basis of the quantity of information weighted according to the behavioral relevance (a negative correlation). The fact that humans are at least slightly aware of the basic operating principles of attention can be inferred from the characteristic conflict observed in everyday interactions. As Solso suggests, the generation of attention fields allows us to consciously perceive only a small subset of the wide range of information that we acquire.

8.4. Balancing Critical Thinking with Standardized Testing

The final chapter comes at a time when educators continue to discuss the extent to which critical-thinking instruction encourages generalization for different content areas and about balance between absorbing curriculum benchmarks and providing instruction that comes at the expense of time spent receiving "real content love". This final chapter reviews relevant research articles that have been incorporated within earlier chapters to suggest additional research ideas for use across multiple grade levels and content areas. Parents engaged many challenges when teaching critical-thinking at home were reviewed. These included challenges when trying to balance the need for limiting the time children spend on digital technology with the potential benefits of using digital technology as a catalyst for acquiring reasoning skills; times when parents didn't have time to provide the explanations and the reviews necessary to maximize the critical-thinking benefit; and times when parents used the parental strategies too frequently, not enough, or the wrong strategy depending on the thinking progression of their respective child.

This concluding chapter has addressed common challenges that arise when using explicit critical-thinking instruction. The topics include the tension between critical-thinking instruction and standardized testing, addressing affective statements within critical-thinking instruction, and the amount of exposure needed for generalization to occur. Each topic has included examples from the elementary level (K-5) to explain specific challenges that could occur within the elementary critical-thinking classroom. Although the K-5 examples only focus on a small piece of critical-thinking instruction, many additional challenges exist for other grades as well. For instance, students not previously exposed to critical-thinking instruction may demonstrate limited interest when the activity is first introduced, questions may quickly become overwhelmingly complex, training students to use similar strategies when solving problems in the natural environment may be difficult, and teachers may need close collaboration with content-area instructors to effectively implement critical-thinking instruction using other content-based processes (e.g., scientific method) that were not addressed here. Challenges also arise in teaching counterargumentation strategies in the writing curriculum, modifying open-ended instruction for use with different grade levels, and training instructors in adaptive strategies for immediate use with generic critical-thinking instruction.

8.5. Promoting Critical Thinking in Online Learning Environments

Educators can develop activities that foster other higher order skills that are beneficial for honest, rigorous, and independent thinking, such as curiosity, creativity, and the ability to cope with uncertainty. We believe that having well-designed assignments with specified procedural and conceptual prompts might benefit critical thinking and its associated skills. However, if students do not have authentic opportunities to use this thinking and these skills inside and outside of higher education, they might not see the value of them. Inhabiting them within a meaningful context can help educators circumvent the trap of promoting procedural or disconnected processes. It also provides students with the decision-making capability to identify the assignment and challenge their own solutions.

Educators might also think about how to create assignments that are adaptable both to different contexts and to the different situations of different students. For example, a web assignment asking students to identify online fraudulent information can be structured in such a way that it can be adapted and performed with a group of high school students in an in situ classroom, an undergraduate group of college students in an online course, or an intergenerational group of elderly students and high school peer tutors in a webinar. Also, the web tool can be adapted to provide multiple scaffolding, differentiation, and feedback for a variety of learners, such as students with disabilities, students lacking familiarity with online environments, or advanced students in the subject.

CHAPTER 7

Conclusion

The purpose of this concluding chapter is to provide educators and parents with targeted ideas—increasingly building on the exploration of specific areas of critical thinking—to effectively design learning opportunities that will help in cultivating critical thinkers. By infusing critical-thinking strategies within subject-specific content areas, especially in the areas representing many of the grand challenges of our time (e.g., health, global warming, and threat from terrorism), learners are engaged in further thought practices with a specific emphasis. These practices tie to and weave through many of the chapters highlighted in previous chapters and aim to prime readers for greater insight and exploration. Providing even more targeted activities within the specific contexts of critical thinking creates a transformative learning experience of ever-increasing depth in thought formation (e.g., Cherry et al. between experiences and critical thinking) within the interconnected domains of content knowledge development, metacognition, and critical thinking.

While this book is designed as a resource for educators and parents, it is also designed for readers interested in improving and enhancing their own critical thinking. Engaging with the tasks, applications, and self-assessment activities throughout the chapters provides opportunities for readers to practice the various phases of the critical-thinking process and to reap the benefits of utilizing critical-thinking strategies. In this final chapter, we present additional strategies to cultivate learners' critical thinking in specific domains and summarize the unique characteristics of two populations discussed in the book: gifted and culturally diverse learners. Strategies presented in this chapter provide learners with opportunities to excel and challenge them to think critically in a variety of settings, as well as to "learn to think new thoughts" (Dewey 1910:145); students explore challenges with an in-depth understanding from exploring ideas from multiple perspectives.